ANSWERLANDS

Joseph Minden is a poet and schoolteacher.
His first collection, *Poppy* (Carcanet, 2022),
was a poetry Book of the Year in the *Daily
Telegraph* and *History Today*, recommended by
the LRB Bookshop, and highly commended
in The Forward Prizes.

Also by Joseph Minden

Poppy (2022)

ANSWERLANDS

JOSEPH MINDEN

CARCANET POETRY

First published in Great Britain in 2025 by
Carcanet
Main Library, The University of Manchester
Oxford Road, Manchester, M13 9PP
www.carcanet.co.uk

A CIP catalogue record for this book is
available from the British Library.

ISBN 978 1 80017 517 4

Book design by Andrew Latimer, Carcanet
Typesetting by LiteBook Prepress Services
Printed in Great Britain by SRP Ltd, Exeter, Devon

The publisher acknowledges financial
assistance from Arts Council England.

CONTENTS

SUMMER

Without hallucinating the child puts out a sample of dream potential and lives with this sample in a chosen setting of fragments from external reality.

D. W. WINNICOTT

The word is a thing in our consciousness, as Ludwig Feuerbach put it, that is absolutely impossible for one person, but that becomes a reality for two.

LEV VYGOTSKY

DIPTYCH

1

There is the church bell tolling
    from the simple steeple.
The cobbles are whale-backed and shining.
The road is a ribbon cast into the valley.
The light is the first spring light
    when it is still winter.

It is morning in the village on a Sunday.

There are no casual and inevitable sounds,
    no routine greetings,
no clatterings of wheels passing over
    the uneven ground.

    What is there?

2

    I begin to lose my voice
but the tall red school still stands
    on my tongue
at the edge of the fen

and somewhere in the building
    high and hidden away
    time comes and goes
        lording it

'PADDOCK CALLS'

FIRST WITCH: I come, Graymalkin.

SECOND WITCH: Paddock calls.

THIRD WITCH: Anon.

MACBETH, Act 1, Scene 1

and fell asleep
the night neverended
spell of a person unsleeving
sweat-yellow
flat on impact in the mattress
the night a tunnel
and so full of dreams
corridors and classrooms
teachers falling from dreams
eye caught on edges
bleeding in
levitating in the heart of night
a pendent bed
suspended up among a
strained extension of thin leaves
that memory
which memory
the warder of the brain
attendant on a fume-horde
semi-faces in whorls of smoke
would light the way to
temple-haunting martlet
winding as ivy
tendril of fairy lights
brittle columns
in the midnight castle
moon
stripped eye
groups the most complex
and mysterious ordeals, there
around the table
abandoned banquet
jawdrop committee
a kind of cantilevered voltage

hanging out over
        objects over thoughts
                fragments or wholes
        eyelashes tears
        tears eyelashes
        I can't come in
                        Miss
I have an eyelash in my eye
    fuck you you fat bitch
        I have a tear in my heart
            I cannot speak
    these eyelashes are stuck

I wake in the dark with half a suit on, the sun coming over the far hill, sleeves in a buttery light. Kat is still sleeping until, at seven, I gather her into my arms, hoist her into the day and step out to the car.

Paddock, send out your tranquility in the surface of water.

Where the place? A heath, Paddock at the edge with her note. A drowsy bank, intricate with flowers. A fen, stretched out in the wordlessness of memory. A school.

A school fringed round with oxlips, violets, wild thyme and honeysuckle. A school built in an old field on the edge of a new town, dressed in ribbons like Mollie the carthorse. In the meadow at the end of the fen. A bespoke facility. A public-private partnership.

A neat grid, marked out in assured white paint. A punctilious grid, the mesh of the fence surrounding the tennis courts. An austere grid, the wide glass windows of the school. An undistinguishable grid, lines trembling in pixels.

A sylvan pagoda; two, three cones; a bag of aggregate.

darkness cycles
in and out
the glass halls
same day eternity, tooled
as if children went on for ever
frogspawn stacked up
that I cannot hide myself
crying on Sunday night
eyes in the small hours
crying on Monday morning
under a structure of blossom
with a hacksaw
and a tape measure
and a heap of memories
good man
struggling man
good man going again
at the speed of fragments
rubble lip of a wave
self-squadron
that scattered
pinned in this centrally
so tired I
cat and asleep
weak in my boxers mid-afternoon
and after that time a comet
rumourous scar
not alone gladly
just gliding stunned
in wire mesh
footnotes

Every morning, I come to a stop before the fence and stare at the chemical blue of the tennis court. They arrive.

Hail. Old friends, doubled. Faces ghoulish in the northern aspect, blushing in the southern. From gorse and fibrous sinews of roots to the wild uncertain rose, light-tongued sweet brier, apple-like, shouldering fragrances. Hail. Hail. Hail.

Hail, old faces, pageant of translucent petals, strains from dual climates. All hail my sisters, dressed in tatters of executive wind. All hail my Cobweb, my Blossom, my Moth, hazy, half-recognised, resurgent. And hail my familiar equivalent, Paddock. There at the edge of the fen.

And wakes it now to look so green and pale? Learning is something that has to be *sustained*. Can it be sustained under such pressure? Paddock distant and unperturbed, waiting like a rock in the middle of a sound.

Finally, in the beginning of spring. Ditchling Beacon, from where you drive down into the sky, coming to every morning levitating on a carpet. From where you drive down onto the multi-coloured pile of mid-Sussex, where golden knights strafe the trees. Thameslink. Tranquility of stupefaction.

But it is only interstitial morning. One of the many trick mornings of the night, niches in the castle wall. And yet I would not sleep, sitting in my car at the tennis court. Suddenly, the grid in the fence. Harmless there. Almost dissolved by sky.

So, into the Resources Room. All hail, colleagues. Moth: the lid of their tupperware. A salad of lettuce and sliced frankfurters. Popping the little pink discs happily into their mouth. Killing swine.

Cobweb swings one leg over another and tucks into their couscous. The graphic novel *Black Hole*. This virus in the background, just a kind of buzz. Mustardseed coughs into their mask. The bell goes and suddenly the room is empty, folded up and slid into the soul.

half a thought to
interview, Colman
blimp inflatable
mustard dummy
over three lakes
hairpin rollicking lawn
no end of dream pageant coming out
haunting the blades and daisies
with theatrics
silly tenacities
the Teach First
dreg squad
small-time Mussolini club
cudgelling your book
into distant damnation
here come the students
of Pimlico Academy
The Petchey Academy
bursting
the wire knives
of their entrainment
Red Cross knight stuck
on his true tears
congregate at the entrance
playing fields chained shut
talk to your friends
the principal discovers himself
an iron thimble
mushroom foreplanted, glade care
Securicor edge
and good thoughts of a coffee shop
too much wig, say, in the face to think
is *this* thought, to that
sandstone faun

blended off pantheon
drones on pudding parade
yolk slopes
conciliatory facades as
whole air vents, grid events
a thousand white electric miniatures
marching over the drawbridge
depression
into the castle
old slow moon
wanes, quickly dreams
away the time
weak sweat
soaked into cotton
washed off and
vanished down the plughole

I have just sat with Mustardseed in the midst of low babble discussing the beautiful violence of fire. Out of the window, dressed in the witching hour's holographic fabric, the tree has thin fingers shaking. Yellow buds. Intermittent sleeves of yellow lichen. Corridors ankle deep in water, everybody wading through the needs of a pupil.

If Friday could be cut open and bleed into permanent stupor; Saturday afternoon in bed with Kat, the real estate agent Knock and Nosferatu. And Cobweb, found driving their keys into their forearms. Crying in lessons. And when you ask why, the grid steps out of your mouth wearing your voice, owle, shrieking his balefull note, violent silhouette in which a rusty knife fast fixed stood, falls dead in the face of their need.

We go down to the sea. Caterwauling weather. Rain is as spray of ghost waves and out there is the moonshine of windmills. Dread's shadow passing, twelve to twelve. All the rivers that sink east out of the island. Monday morning, like an eye opening into a cave.

There is a new pupil in the school today: Count Orlok. Soft waves of panic. Almost like Blossom in the Resources Room looking at red peppers. Numerous times, adults turn right or left through doorways and just keep on falling.

Deposit this howl in me, Sir Palomides. O, my armour is heavy and the bough of this yew tree cushiony hard.

try out my teeth on
                get sorry
factory pastry, that bitter
        conveyor-drawn carriage
            intricate, post-ball
        flake comedown
vista that conceals in levels
            burns rushing
        out of the clients' ears
            such their gianthood
        single-growth courthouses
aptitude and ermine trim
        the central civic highway
            students on exam benefits
assessments on life support
        the Duke of Edinburgh
tossing in the furrowed sheets
        out of the dark-bright dark
                fore-white
            green castle
mossy oak shifting its limb
        with some tower of sword
    pearlness on the paintwork
        where the maid who
un-ate the chicken's balance lives
    in discord with her master
    ever sharpening the knife
            like the bed is the sea
        I keep massing up
        breaking apart
        tempest-tossed
    saturated later on
            brainsickly

the word is the same
when I can't do this
you heath-hags, serrated sisters
night a rag from off your backs

And step out into a sudden clearing. A feast of colours all around. Hermia, Helena, Lysander and Demetrius sleeping on, undisturbable. The moon falls off, all fringes of pearlescent petal sluiced to the derivative of rainbow, pooling in the overripe bower of the bald goblins, their colour lassoos. I am inside a tremulous memory. Slow odour of boiling sugar.

I am walking around the classroom handing out metaphors in a sky-blue suit. Terrible conversation on the phone just now, squatting between cars. Can you die of fear? Fine moorland scenery. Magnificent coastline. Dreams all literally true.

No, Sir. I don't want her eyes were fireflies. I want the sky is a mask.

again, again
it was the owl that shrieked
that fatal bellman, yes
the faceless bird, uplifting
a pink waterfall from the neck
backlit somewhere, yes
a tree I would
a mountain call but two lights
in the castle wall, Mustardseed
shouting mouthless
in the stair dark, what looks like
reluctance, matter of this child of
computer screens, that this
morning I was at the bridge
trying to kill myself
Sir
disciplined vortex, simple
mesh before the court
the one with the lightbulb
head carrying a glacier
in a plastic bag
through the scrub
by the railway, singing
wordlessly, in swinish sleep
of this writing hand, of pistons
triode valves, half-memories
in framework for the mad
attachment, eyeball
exploder, as light from
a prism marks out this
box in your skull, sick
very, very steep
so fall forward, blank faces

in rows randomising through
the mesh, drought conditions
then rain, like others
have witnessed situations
far worse, rain on eyeball
inverse passing flower

Paddock begins singing wordlessly. That there is some message. But not *message*. Some mesh of potential meaning. With give. A language we cannot unearth between us. Leather jacket and the warmth of hands. The babbling love of the sisters I have. My sisters. Whom I have not seen in a long time. Whom I have not seen with my eyes. Come the dead landscape, Greymalkin.

Wednesday again. Moth stands up, swings on their rucksack, gives me the finger as they go out the door and is NOT. FUCKING. COMING. BACK. Still as they fledd, their eye was backward cast. As if their feare still followed them behynd. Some days a charge in school. The wind. The pull of the moon.

Sir, I don't know what to say. Why might you want a border between fairy land and the world of the human lawmakers?

That orange front coming out of the dawn. The lovers in the wood turning entirely red. The bewitched evening sitting on my log with its basket of changelings.

Create your own familiar. Mine rides on a tortoise. Flies, in fact. But soft. What?

Mine is a formal path. Mine has Gucci flip flops. Mine has a spliff. Mine is posh with a malicious side. Mine has dinosaur arms. Mine is a judo master. Mine fits in with the woods. Mine can teleport. Mine has no attributes but this small, red picture. Mine has six types of face including a floating circle and a floating circle, two biro slashes. Mine has a black eye because someone crushed his car with a tank. Mine has just given someone a parking ticket, hence his white suit.

Mine parts the curtain of the present classroom with a foot. Beyond its fringed realism is a fen. A glade. A circle of sleeping elements. Human wheat limp at the heart-side. And from that other side I look back in.

Peaseblossom. Milk-white head. White denim. White Nikes. White polo shirt. Walking through the school with four pints of milk lanced from my sclera with a razor.

up the ladder I did
grope, some sadness
element, almost
like a shadow, pollen
phantom in the car-shaped head
a standard model
what, you sit up from
your reverie, your hand back
there, brown grease
Sir, I'm going
to cut myself, can I
go out, the fence a net
of low and
swollen cloud, bloated
but can get no fuller
one thing, or two
his uncle died in the night
he looked a bit sad this morning
the assessment, forcing treasury
tags through sheafs of
sockets, dawn shining
into the oven, wind
a tree, throwing
itself from self to self
the day one bluebell stooped
over everything, staring
eyeless at the blood
it handles
radiant against no surface
murder of its lightcast
knife

Tuesday again. No one cares. Work harder. Tear it all down. Tuesday again. And when you rip its photograph – wire. Again. My eyes phase suddenly to gauzes you push blood through. Yes, and all this in a Citroen Berlingo, in a simple car park, with that spectral vehicle body head.

Snowglobe in my pocket, I walk into the Humanities corridor trying to keep it down. We know that to keep people working, drill their tongues to the desk. Peaseblossom slouches against a wall of lockers, an ash-grey cloud. Hard to remain real in the face of their disdain. Every other student a voiceless tower.

Huge feelings stalk the corridors. Cobweb sprawls by the toilets, their phone gone. Their mind scattered like ice. All about them wandring ghostes did wayle and howle. A gaggle of scared teachers posturing from a distance.

I haven't cried at work in years. The feeling of marking snowballing. Six hundred scripts a week. Eleven of us. Sometimes the week is endless. Every day, the week. That is why you open broom cupboards and find teachers crying. And after the reverberations have passed on, the vulnerability of the body in peace.

Hush. With a whole class. Among the musk roses and the reremice. Cobweb waiting in the doorway like a puddle. The smile is the front edge of an axe-head of terror. It quickly turns into a brow-cloud and showers. What has my mouth in it but air and nothing. Back to the attic. Try again tomorrow.

But, if the simplicity of my face could walk out into the clearing kept behind the falsehood of the day, the surgical accusation of the classroom would dissolve. Encounter not shot up with gangways. The mind walking through itself, self-possessed and rightly multiplied. Paddock.

Wednesday, a shield
in the forehead, knowing that
sleep is one thing
sleep hath murdered
sleep, that feeling of despair
when sleep has been all
peeled
come, the day will be
soon done, time and the hour
run through, when
what you see's a time
for quiet exhalation
wandering about and bumping in
to one another, Wednesday
again, fuck you, the people
driving in as
clockwork, factoids, wind
of shit and bingo every lesson
hang around until I have to go
the last time
outside, dandelion pieces
dandled on the wind, the wide windows
then a tiny portion
of a globe, where the place
a heath, a glade fringed
with musk roses
eglantine, wild thyme
with hyperspeed wind, seeds
all time and out into the furrows of
the skin of sleep

And fell asleep, the night neverended. One tower in unabridged nighttime and the counterweight, familiar, like a heron reeded in stark silhouette. A second tower, slender and humane.

Friday again. Pallet. Same arrivals on their clocks. Staring at the grid. All the gaps make a face but who? Green tendencies forced through a wire gauze.

Moth slipped the remote from the desk and pranked me for ten minutes, switching the projector off every time I put it on. They sat wordlessly as I flapped, looking to freeze the screen. In their mind the addictions of their parents were on, and on, and on. But their laughter really was reaching for intimacy. Their muteness was the sound of words abandoned in one place alone.

So you discover I have more strength than you think. Only the surface gives in terror as if to die. Beyond that is the lasting resonance of my opposite face. Kind shield. A satellite that returns in silence what gives words sound.

Dusk comes to the edge of passable terrain. Whose voice is this speaking now? When you were a baby, I looked at you, wondering. That voice, like a dome. There you were, sometimes losing touch with the sphere I inhabit. Never looking at my face. Without eyes for my face.

Driving constantly over the landscape of settling terror.

AUTUMN

Twenty years later, I'd
  forgotten my key.

  In the dark of my pocket
in the cottage front garden

time loops with a broken
  surface. I reach out and

  ring. Alice opens the door
and hands me the spare.

Just her hand, mind,
  white against the night room.

Levitating in the infinite
    well shaft of sleep
  I can't close my eyes.

  A black doorway
full of model apples,
    fingertips

      of hibiscus,
   the black orchard floor
and his hand's phantom tree.

I still see how he reversed
    through the breeze
  blocks, into the school hedge.

Having observed the lesson
the inspector presumed to pass
judgment on Danielle:
you're a bright girl
but you're being led.
Our eyes met
in the conspiracy of children
which says
who the fuck is that
and smiles off, distracted
like a slide
into the afternoon.

When I make my new
friend, now
as this eleven-year-old
I discover –
suddenly –
his mouth doesn't
stop but leads
on and on,
his relentless approach
immortalised
by the loop of time.
Get it away!

Saying
you're dead to me
(I discover as the inspector)
is an important type of
murder. I, too, retain

the infinity
of starting out as a human
but it is *mine*. I cannot bear
to know better.
Or you
of the asking,
the asking again.

Midday sun falls into the church
where green and orange rearrange
and orange. A child's head floats
in a pew. Cups of tea arrive
and take their leave. Smiles,
the face of the village.
Without, or

walking up the lane
is muffin (wrapped
in a flag) apple
(the nature
of harvest) and
(pretty camouflaged)
huge rules.

Arrived. The hum of the fan at two frequencies sounds like Pauline Oliveros. October blows in without compunction. No-one can be close to anyone else.

The school has been dismantled and reconstructed chronologically so that the first minute of the day takes a thousand years. What forest shields its hillside from the stare of the sea?

When you come into these logical corridors it is hell you think about. Quiet as the hum of infinite fans. Hell, quietly.

I am standing water,
    teach me to flow;
the waves only crash
    where the rocks let them go.

The rocks only live
    in the arms of the sea;
the sea is not certain,
    neither are we.

Look at the foam
    on the crest of the waves;
the healing that ruins,
    the ruin that saves.

From two
eyeballs (both
mine) being
squashed until
they pop, I
make out her father's
arrest, the anniversary
of his dad's suicide,
crisp packets
blown into grovelling.

Cheese squares
face-plant from
their bread clamp;
real hunger is
everywhere just pairs
of eyes looking
out from impulse
tanks, no
improper, too-early
decorum.

Inside dialogue
where fear dies

these strange heads up to
an internal face that is not from

inside, where the court of encounter
sits with its pulses as words.

Paddock smiles on but when she speaks
it is with a mouth full of day, thick hiss

no burn.

I'm lying in bed
looking through
the sweet, shattered
pane of nighttime.

Bring it back.
Bring back
the sweet, shattered
pane of nighttime.

The two-tone Pauline Oliveros hum continues, flooded with adrenaline. Teachers flit to classrooms, arms swinging from yesterday to tomorrow and tomorrow.

Jane, eating a tuna salad, is on to someone else about – there is a constant alertness. Everything is being thrown at us. It's unsustainable. And that side of it you couldn't fault. I feel exhausted. Exhausted. I'm doing so much of it outside of school. So much of it.

I want that time again with different hours. The leaves with autumn brown hanging in falling. Gone down home down blossom through. Soon grown. Cut off. Regrown, returned and gone. Red berries already looping ripe into the underfoot crush on Melbourne Place.

The institution doesn't
give their lives
nothing, slipping
into county lines,
the rarity of
humans. Go now
to that other classroom,
as forms begin
to haze into their
colours. Everything,
Scrooge included,
crowds to break.
Go to your
brain for ever more,
sometimes flying,
buried as a tree. Whom
shall I send, and who will go
for us? The children
are a constant lament.

Last spring, the three of us
knee-deep in evening,
in the dew pond,
stopped. This spring,

in pond array,
    like thought,
neither forcing
    nor retreating,

we lean, as if to push
the thing and, as a body
in our thought, say
        there.

At this moment, the class writes
perfectly. They are absorbed,
genuinely wrapped up,
some of them putting down their pen
to leaf through a dictionary
or to look at a scene in the play.

If this is authoritarian – and
it is – the startling thing is it's
so gentle. Everyone is busy
and no-one looks sad. The room
is peaceful. I think the line
to cease upon the midnight
with no pain. The sea is
outside. The ceiling panels
form a grid. Sometimes
students look that way
as they pause and think

and continue to write
perfectly.

Kat and I, walking against
the river, the simple path detailed
with complex frost, observed
Reading's toadish Thames-dreams
frittering out, boathouses jaw-deep
in water. Trains iced Tilehurst's
black embankment; we were
infants against the citadel wall.
The law doesn't care what you
intend, said Kat, intent's complexity
resolving to the simplicity
of text, the frantic, although stately,
scatterwork of nude branches
mopping and mowing through the
dayglass. Complex blossom,
simple, bloody cherry. You press
yourself outwards, that simplicity
against the texture of the world,
the world as what it is. A Tempest,
flown in corkscrews
high above the white, arrested
fields. Berries blown out, dressed
with a lingering drop and red by frosty
clearings; nighttime lasting
unbroken in its graveyards
into the day. At Pangbourne, Anna
rooted from a Nissen hut, turning
English; Poland receded into
the shade of beech and ash. Simple
seedling, complicating radicle.
And then, in Whitchurch, arcane village

intonations over apple cake'and coffee
in the charity café – her flat is dark,
where is she now? – sounded merely
flat, the carpet complicated
with crumbs. Kat won a hot water bottle
in the raffle. Thank you, Anna –
farewell. What does it take
to feel at home? I asked above
the Thames. Flatness in the eyes,
the complex eyes, Kat offered.
Something unsuspicious in their
slick, barracked
in the simple dark. Blackcoat.
Hardwick. A pillbox
sailing by. Daylight bruising
bluer, chestnut mush, the river
steaming in constricting air, mouths,
self-thought benign,
yawning questions into disturbed
scenery. A boathouse gaped
into itself, cosy, though cold,
in dereliction, like a flooded
hearth. I must just look at this,
said Kat. Die Brust
des Einfache; die anspruchsvolle
Vielgestalt. Ice-reperfected,
bolted with displaced nighttime,
in a white thinned by the dusk,
a ruined mansion
watched the pathway turn to Goring,
Moulsford, Wallingford.
Look at that, Kat said.
What is it?

They've kettled the kids
said Suzanne, turning again
from the toilet block.

If I can just make this one thing not die,
the clappers in the loft will stop their murders.
    A spur of the river, the bargemen.
        Downpour, springshine.
A Hue Walker through the reeds coming.
        Floodable garden.
        Wheatish flame
         past the casement guttering.
I have been here a thousand years,
a time before my head formed a house
        threaded by bluebottles.

        Livewell,
        Bidenmorta.
        Bread oven,
         shovel called peels.
That amazing bread oven.
That huge bed of courgettes.

        Continent,
        Lovegod.
        Greene carpet.
        Brand irons, a pair
of creepers, fire, shovell, tongs
and bellowes. Sour milk and chalk.

Rammed chalk. Chalk laid and rammed
        down, milk poured over.
    Initially, a layer of mould over,
      gradually died back,
still areas of green mould on the floor where

the daylight is strongest, feels soft,
looks right but is dead,
no hot core,
downs the visible top layer of chalk,
deepens upon chalk,
moisty,
the wet bone of stones.

Who's that sulking in the corner there?
Long Laurence,
Nine Men's Morris,
inscrutable gridwork kept in the chest,
Thomas Cromwell till he fell out of favour
and slept under a juniper tree:
behold, then
an angel touched him,
did quite well,
son of gentry,
a cake baked on the coals,
and a cruse of water at his head.

The villagers hate me for my love of timber,
the fact that when I cry I shed thatch
and out fumes sooty smoke.
The oak leaf in the corner,
that's a bit of history.
A sprig of oak leaves chosen by my uncle,
Joseph Armitage,
I don't know but
not long after the Great War.

Like a tamping rod blown through the eyebase,
England watched aghast, France became
a sea of black flags.

Rats that survived became flea towns,
evidence of the lifestyle at Brighton,
    Napoleon-faced syphilis,
    an upsurge of village,
        omega-shaped,
    grown over with bye-laws.
    A garderobe?
Fumigate,
        yes.

First, the property at Barmouth in Wales,
        Octavia,
        Robert
and Hardwicke in hands,
    a posy trinity.
Then, yes, the second, Alfriston,
a yeoman farmer, naturally built.

Who's that limping along the lucid Cuckmere?
The Rev. Fred, that undaunted conservationist -
    the villagers thought him mad;
        Robert Witt:
        out sprang The Art Fund,
        The Courtauld,
some deposit from the First Chimurenga;
    the ham Earl of Dorset, spluttering;
    commissioners of sewers, muttering;
        dearest verycoast,
            typically mute,
    after the kinges high way to Seaford,
    reed-dragging his crested pole.

From the start, a quilt
of radical socialists,
key establishment figures,
traditional landowners
and the Royal Family.
A powerful vision,
its vagueness
its power.

We would, naturally, be asked to restore it,
no indigenous collection, a collaboration
to dress the room,
rather a poser if they mean what then to put it to,
spindly bed frame limp with bonnet curds,
crumpet stale as plastic,
looping letters,
one corner of a central meadow,
twisted spire,
and a ladder to heaven for ever,
river outfall,
the ruynes of an ancient chapple.
Harriet,
keeping chickens in a hollow tree.
Older versions, titans buried under the hill.

Fences adored.
Haunters of silences.
My tongue,
pen
and paintbrush combined.
I have just heard from Mr Loftus Brock.
The present is so obviously imaginary.
Bring out your dead.

COMMON

At some point, Kat would appear
in her green coat
walking beneath Cutter Ferry bridge,
the threshold from which Seth,
a different god,
approaches.
Life becomes increasingly sacred
in the privacy of its signs,
the forms mythologised by fog
on Stourbridge Common. All that
cometh is vanity, almost
five thousand years
gone and then Fen
Ditton. Some of us are taken
long inside, fixed to a statement
like a small, golden dragon –
I am evil –
mysteriously animate,
recurrent for attention,
more easefully present and
softer than most memory.
On Christmas Day, a psalm took
Kat. Let the sea make a noise,
and all that therein is. This
lasted until
now. I was taken, too,
but by the singing:
one man singing there,
against the whitewashed wall,
for thirty years, the glass
clear but centred on coloured

figures. Full
hours do not die
emptied. Satisfy us early.
Little St Mary's emptied out
into the warm noon,
the disintegration of Cambridge,
hedgerows, fenland
darkness, Black
Shuck. The next day,
Kat set off along the river.
Small bombs in a cold haze
traced Seth. There was, as always,
a Fair wherein should be sold
trinkets, notions,
Silver, Gold.
Only strangers came and went
under the bridge.

SPRING

DREAMLAND 1

There is
a theme park
I have heard of.
Mist rises
from shallow water
in the early morning.
A cow stands
ankle-deep
in the flood,
the scenic railway
oopses
into the sand drifts,
and the Temeraire
dissolves
into a waterwheel,
a magnificent sunset
and borderless waters.
I see it now.

It is Epiphany, when
we reflect on how things are
revealed to us. With masks
back, their eyes come
forward harder from
around the room, but widen
with what they can't say.

They are subdued, deprived
of the impulsive
preliminaries to expression:
how the mouth moves
often so immediately after
where the eyes go.
On their own, the eyes are legless.

Year 8 and I are thinking together.
Where do tears start? Inside
these eyes. And where do they end
up? Below them. So that, by
definition, they lower
you, those characters,
into the world.

CORRIDOR FRAGMENT

After a swimming trip, Dafydd drew a smiling stick figure completely surrounded by graphite water, an inch beneath the waterline, choked in what looked like stone.

That doesn't seem much like your nice outing, said Mrs Brading, pointing instead at Hannah's bright blue crayon pool with five pink, happy faces floating safe, alive and decapitated in the paper-white air.

I am not yet old enough to make decisions. My knees stick out of my legs at the back of the classroom. Small plastic chair. Triangles of Semtex in my sandwich.

Hobbled on my
home boulder in the river
no sane person above the baby level
does. As the fine-grained grids
rub together, I –
sprinkled out
a species refined as
pink salt.

By
the water flows.
By: a little fingertip,
a red toe. Dip and
dip, bringing up
drippingly forged seconds and
eventually
a finger, pointing

at the falls a small way on.
Between their near horizon
and distant roar
is the nothing
time
towards which the gloss
of direction invents
everything's loss.

w/c 17 January

after reading Tom Leonard's 'Being a Human Being'
at poetry club

Alinafe stopped at the line
not to keep one's mouth shut
to hold onto one's job.

I find this weird because
I don't know why you would keep
your mouth shut to hold onto

someone else's job. I explained
that this was about one
and the same person. I nodded

but later said again, I don't know
why you would keep your mouth
shut to hold onto someone

else's job. I went home
understanding how understanding
is about desire.

I would be a tyrant to force
two things into one
like eyes, side by side.

Pelagian latitude:
that we are able to see with our eyes
is no power of ours. Sparse
blares. It all begins
with the central yellow
of the lemon: a modest,
even retiring,
focal point, set before
a fluted glass jar,
tablecloth white,
clock blue. He's
suddenly direct
in the disclosure of serious
things. A muscular conch
introduces pinks,
faint oranges,
a deep, suggestive red.
The tablecloth glows,
a panic-stricken face
displayed through a second
face, with a
removed pink and
non-committal orange.
The coffee cup beside
the conch, divided
from the lemon
by a strip of midnight blue,
is immaterial, assembled
merely out of nearby
colours, running to
dupe the lookers;

he glances at me
furtively. The other
strangely fugitive
aspect of the composition
is the featureless darkness
to the far right. The Met
called last night;
his brother is again in
prison. Only
the yellow in the centre is
purely and vividly
uninterested in disguise,
almost surreal and
supernatural
in his simplicity
and presence.

At poetry club, we
were discussing the word
crust. A disgusting
word. Feet,
wounds, scabs,
bread
and the earth.

With half the department
sick and thunder,
lightning or rain,
I need
to shut my
eyes and it
is the thing there.

The pulse
of attention,
a heartbeat larger
than the room,
registers
in surges
of an entrant wind.

the feeling of mess
as words come through the faces
wild, dumb to the ear
the inward rooting of together
refusing and refusing and
the earring
purple diamante dinosaur
squeals, jerks
a blade winking
from under a cushion
do – and when do
the eyes all look together
the difficult ones going
or on their way out

Factory lettering –
C. Dugard Machine Tools Ltd –
passes off inside a blink.
That was ten minutes ago
on the Old Shoreham Road.
Now, shallow flags. Paddock
out to sea, banner-smiling
with the carefree wind blowing through,
enough for everyone. School's
out, its last day
up the Fort. Instead, thin
Southwick Beach, where
Charles II off-esquiffed
the bacon of his bap,
my bap,
a breasted sail
flapping in the breeze like a
cavalier scarf. Cheerio
Sussex, shame
of Worcester. A few folk
drinking tea in the mouths
of workshops, assessing
the day. Cross the glistening
lock. Thank you.
Pleasure.
Ships bigger than thought could fit
in Suez, Littlehampton
by the small shore,
big chimney, bendy
bacon girder, the whole grid
losing tenure, canvas-googling

with glisten
into my mouth, bright foam
applauding into the eager
    shingle, elderly
couples looking decades
    into each other,
the dream of freedom
a bracket of that love.

Get in. Park. Day coming up. Foot of the field – the windmill.
A dream obelisk dissolving into daylight, non-negotiables,
responsibilities.

A young kid, Year 7, Year 8, squatting in the grass, waiting too.
Is he bracing himself or is he made up?

The grid is composed of the lines between reassurance and
disfigurement. All my childhood.

w/c 6 March

On Karen's apron
rhubard and custard, bloodshot
stitches like tailings.

Peter and James fell into
the bottom of a lift shaft

I vaguely saw them crunched there
in this glass bore

Slowly
the firemen came as paramedics

There was a brief
muffled investigation

Peter is dead they said
coming back up to the rest of us

The smallest hesitation that
Peter is truly but not indefinitely dead

Hello spine
ladder to turn out

The same place in that is what
stairs are up to the top suite

DREAMLAND 2

I see it now.
There is
a spinning wheel
from the highest chamber
        in the turret
    on top of the cupboard.
    It is
    accessible
by your hair,
        Rapunzel,
    by baby barrel,
        mummy barrel
and daddy barrel,
    by a door ajar,
        a beanstalk,
        ladder,
    and by my little eye
at the glassless window.

DR FOX
After Afanase'ev

Something priceless must
have left the world, old man.
Why else would you cry like this,
sitting in the road rather than
soldiering on, kicking up red dust

with others making
the journey? What is it?
The fox stooped, tendering his
questions. I'll sit here for a bit.
What's in this bag? Is the weight taking

it out of you? No.
Don't ask. The pale man stared
weakly at his feet, aghast;
the fox had a quick look. Prepared
for something dull, his eyes widened so

much at what he saw
he turned away and coughed.
This was some windfall breakfast.
A bag full of pulped up meat, soft
flesh on the bone, pieces of a poor,

smashed person. The fox
took a breath. This gory
meal must be mine. What's my route
to this feast? I need the story
of his sadness first, of how the rocks,

stock-still, came to dash
apart a soul so dear
to him but, in this, pick fruit
from catastrophe for me. Tear
after tear hit the dirt. A bright rash

had flared in their tracks
on the man's cheeks. Come, old
friend, tell me. A burden shared
is halved or sometimes, so I'm told,
demolished altogether. Relax.

Breathe deeply. Speak, said
the fox, tougher in tone
but also as if he cared.
The man leant down and took a stone
from the tear-wet path. My wife is dead

but my sorrow's start
was small, no bigger than
this pebble: a cabbage sprout.
Look over there, quite far off. Can
you make out the enormous green dart

rooted in that plot
but shot to the sky's edge?
How it streaks up, almost out
of sight? That piece of mutant veg
flew up this morning, opened the spot

you just catch if you
strain your eyes: the black star
of a hole in heaven's heights.
Like a green scar extending far
across otherwise unblemished blue,

it stretched above them.
At a black dot, its arc
ended. The man moaned. By rights
I should be rich. Beyond that dark
puncture are treasures: I climbed the stem

and looked through the gap.
I could never have dreamt
of the vast, unexplained wealth
I saw. Gold? Trying to pre-empt
him, the fox misfired. A sudden snap

of sorrow: it cost
me the love of my life.
The fox, regrouping with stealth,
was understanding. Your poor wife –
you must have tried to take her up, lost

your grip at the top.
He laid out his red paw
consolingly on the man's
knee, but under his coat the claw
curled. Tell me the whole story, don't stop.

Let out your deep grief
speaking. What did you see,
from beyond this plant that spans
the sky, to make your wife ready
to risk ascent to the highest leaf?

Sob-hollowed and spent
the man calmed down, went on.
Yesterday, I bought a sprout
and, according to convention,
planted it: plenty of water sent

into its small roots,
bedded under the warm
ash in the firm hearth earth, out
of reach of the threat of the storm
and safe, in good time, to bear its fruits.

Then I went to bed
and dreamt strangely. A whiff
of leaf stirred me. All I know
is I yelled and my wife woke, stiff
into a meringue of sheets, her head

cramped by sudden leaves.
And there was me shouting:
if the plant doesn't get through
it'll ruin the house. Outing
it, though, meant climbing onto the eaves

and tearing off tiles
from the roof. I cleared six
and stuck my arm in, a blind
periscope after the apex
of the growth. More to the left – you're miles

away, my wife called,
guiding the search. I caught
it, pulled it across to find
the hole I'd made and, briefly, thought
I'd saved the day. But, freed, the sprout stalled

for a still second,
seemed to pause, and then smashed
into the sky with force stored
up overnight. Of course, I crashed
groundwards hard – I was sure death beckoned,

it was a big fall
from the height I was at
and the momentum that floored
me had explosive malice. Flat
on the earth, I was ready to wail:

my wife was done for,
surely. The sudden burst had
obliterated the house,
levelled the walls like they were bad
props. But she'd escaped, debris on her

clothes, face, in her hair.
We watched the cabbage ride
skyward, me and my spared spouse
fast in each others' arms, mouths wide,
heads bent right back, almost unaware

that our home had been
destroyed. We saw the high
birds punched out of broad flight like
botched staples, taken fully by
surprise. The sky became a blue screen

unstitching along
some hidden seam that proved
it green underneath. The spike
of the sprout's tip drove on up, moved
with pure, motiveless purpose, a wrong

vitality, past
the staid clouds and closer
and closer to the bright sun,
a claggy yolk, yellow loser
in the face of mounting speed. At last,

us both prompt to burst
with held breath, the streak stopped,
sounding the stud noise of one
huge, distant, cosmic, semi-popped
balloon and a world-historic first –

that hole in the sky.
The silence settled. Can
that really be a hole in
the sky? my wife wondered with an
uneasy half-laugh, shutting one eye

to bring it into
focus. I think it is,
I replied, adrenaline
flushing me eager with a fizz
of resolve to climb up and look through.

I'll investigate,
I announced. For God's sake,
be careful, said my wife. There
was nothing she could do to make
me stay. Had I only known her fate

the way things went,
I'd have left the stark, black
star to preside in peace where
it hung. Instead, despite my lack
of fitness, I began the ascent.

The stalk's fibrous sides
were easy to grip, its
leaves made good pit stops and I'll
never forget, though all my wits
were to scatter, the strength I felt – tides

of drive seemed to roll
through me, moved by the draw
of that new, celestial
entrance: lunar, not stellar, law
governing, even taking control.

It was a long climb
and I kept passing scraps
of old house, pots, a little
icon showing the Virgin, wraps
of linen looping the leaf stalks. Time

passed. The air grew thin.
I thought of Jack, human
ant, chased for his white, brittle
bones by a giant. Stranger than
fiction, here I was being pulled in

to a tale. Fields turned
into brief squares, roads slight
gossamer. I didn't see,
I was fixed on where the daylight
died above me. My whole body burned.

The hole seemed to surge
towards my rising face.
I leapt. The shadow met me,
stained my features like a surface
of water – I had a strange, strong urge

to laugh, balanced, rapt
at the cabbage's tip,
leaning with one hand aching
up and out, my head at the lip
of the known universe. The fox clapped

his jaws together.
What's hidden in that place?
he gasped, not even faking
curiosity. Boundless space,
and, suspended throughout the ether,

thousands of millwheels
extending beyond sight,
turning and, as they rotate,
regularly throwing out bright
loaves. I caught one. You know when bread feels

just right, light, but has
brittleness in the crust
that can prick you? How I hate
bread, thought the fox, but grinned and thrust
out his tongue like he loved it too: as

I live and breathe – *wow*,
he said out loud. There's more,
said the man. My pupils pooled,
drawing the darkness off the store –
pans of milk, fresh from some flawless cow,

to moisten the bread:
the perfect complement.
I perched there, staring, and drooled,
overwhelmed by this heaven-sent
pension, ticket to an ever-fed

dotage, a vaultless
wonder-warehouse buttressed
by the sweep of the cabbage.
Remembering the loaf, I pressed
its crust, split in and partook. Faultless.

Disappointed by
the lack of flesh or cash
in this miracle storage
cave, factory and divine cache,
the fox returned his sly and hungry

mind to the slick, fresh
joints in the tragic sack,
which meant hearing the next part
of the story. When you got back
to your wife and earth – what then? the flesh

not missing from on
high but there, tasty, close
at hand, prompted him to start.
Like a terrible repeat dose
of the fact that his wife was all gone,

the question reduced
the man to sobs again
and he squashed his head hard south
into his hands as though the pain
required his palms be introduced

through his eye sockets
and his brain seized. Vowels
of grief forced open his mouth,
veering uselessly to howls,
not words. The fox searched in his pockets

for a handkerchief –
at least deal with the snot,
he thought – and rolled out the next
phase of his plan: don't curse your lot,
it may be that I can bring relief.

The man wiped the glaze
off his upper lip, trance
of sorrow broken, perplexed
by the fox's coy assurance.
It depends on how your story plays

out, the fox explained,
so tell me the rest, brave
the memory. Very faint,
the words: I'd give my life to save
hers. In his head, the fox mocked this strained

claim. I know you would,
he lied, like an advert.
The man took up his complaint:
from the top, I saw my wife skirt
the base, staring up, anxious for good

news. I took one last
look at the firmament
of bread and milk, then I stowed
the loaf I held safe for descent
and began the downward climb as fast

as I could, thinking
about how she'd react
when I reached the ground and showed
her what I'd found. I made contact
with the red earth, cried out, ran blinking

into her arms. What
did you find there? she asked,
as though fresh from an ill dream
of her own. I took a pause, basked
in her wonder. Wonders you would not

believe, I beamed. Fat
loaves flung cooling from wheels
and pans of rich, divine cream,
infinitely set out for meals,
as if heaven were nothing but that.

Her sweet expression,
her wide open mouth: the
weak memory's fading, pale
fake's all I've left, along with a
corpse in a heap, what the aggression

of bare gravity
and rock made of her. Straight
away she wanted to scale
the heights too, attain the strange gate,
witness the stock in the cavity.

She picked up a bag
from amongst the scattered
remnants of our house and jumped
in, foetal, scrunching the tattered
brim round her head. Haul me up like swag!

she shouted, muffled
by hessian but full
of adventure. My heart pumped
hard: I felt too tired to pull
myself up the stalk, strangely ruffled

by this weird order
from my packaged wife, scared
that an extra load would be
beyond too heavy if I dared
try a second climb to the border

between plenitude
and the world. But to lose
face in the moment of glee
and triumph would have been a bruise
to my ego. It seems all too crude

now, apprehending
my selfish compulsion,
self-evident as rubble,
but it served then for propulsion:
I raised her, turned back to the bending

plant and remounted.
One hand is worse than two,
half much better than double
the weight in luggage, for those who
climb. I couldn't even have counted

on superior
skill and iron fitness,
as you know, but the inlet
let me down too, no dark largesse
gifting magnetism any more

like the first time tried,
its strange gift overcome
by physical limit, sweat,
the loosening grip of my numb
fingers in the fibre of the side

and bone-white where my
wife depended on them.
The hole just hung, impassive.
My lungs crackled, threw up some phlegm
from the rack of breathing. I nearly

choked on a shatter
of coughs the clot provoked,
slipped sharply, felt my hand give,
my wife slip an inch, silent, cloaked
in sack. She called out: what's the matter?

still calm, but fearful.
Nothing, I came back but
looked down talking and the height
hit me, land a nausea, cut
with unflat furrows, hedgerows. Tearful

with panic and shock,
unriveted by strange
attraction, I swung back, right
over open nothing; the change
in how I balanced made the sack rock

wider out still and
it was harder to keep
pinned in with my nails paring
flesh from the plant's stalk and the sweep
of the bag out searing the bag-hand,

forcing my gaze up.
I let her go because
I saw the black blot staring,
noiseless, for the devil it was
in the good sky, damn the loaf and cup

of milk, the both damned,
evil like a desert
fraudulence. I let her go.
She dropped. I couldn't reassert
the will to grip in time. When she slammed

into earth, a fleck
from where I was, I still
took a few seconds to know
that a fall from such a height will
kill. I came down. You found me, a wreck.

Strategically,
fox let there be silence,
a moment's seeming tribute,
then brought his false balm to the tense
aporia of conclusion. I

am a doctor, known
far and wide for my skill.
As he began to compute
this, the man's eyes started to fill
with hope. In my career, I have shown

that every scourge
that gruesomely afflicts
animal bodies is game
for curing, from the derelict's
creeping sores, to fevers of the verge

of dying, to death's
trusted confidence trick
itself. There's no ill you'd name
that I couldn't mend. Let me pick
up your wife, re-fuse her bones with breath's

unifying rush
and return you to joy
where you saw only mourning,
the long horizon. I'll destroy
her destruction and pull back life's blush.

At this, the man grabbed
the fox's coat with low
sounds of excitement, fawning
in his face: do this, and I'll owe
you everything, anything, he blabbed,

work, love, praise, money.
This, in particular,
is an easy death to fix –
that's why I asked details of her
demise. Bring me some oats and honey.

Then, I need to treat
her in private, behind
the plant. Everything clicks
into place in peace and shade. Kind
fox, said the man. The gift of this feat

will transform the rest
of my life. Let me get
oats. He went over the fence
to call on his neighbour, his wet
cheeks drying and his mind full of best

possible worlds, hope
restored. Doctor fox stood
by the coming succulence,
staring at it; the ordered food
was brought, wrapped in cloth and tied with rope.

He posed as solemn
as possible as he
took the bundle and then picked
up the heavier and bloody
sack, moving off towards the column

the plant made, doubled
under the bulk. He looked
tiny beneath the load, licked
his lips discreetly, the uncooked
feast soon due; the man was untroubled,

keen with awakened
faith. The fox – nose, trunk, tail –
entered the shadow that lay
over the fields like a cold nail,
leaving the day to the wind-governed

trend of smoke rising
from placid chimneystacks
in the vague, abiding way
of the countryside, where an axe
will always split, at unsurprising

intervals, kindling
in some distant, wood-stocked
yard. After a while had passed,
the man began to think he'd clocked
up too long there. His patience dwindling,

against instruction,
he went to determine
if his wife was yet recast
in corrected, unbroken skin
as per the promised resurrection.

How do the people
who name the animals
    pick the names?
asked Frank, accidentally
returning to Eden. Pig.
    Horse.
    Cow. We were
talking about slavery
but his question hung
    inside the subject,
    a bubble inside
a bubble. I had to screech
    into an alleyway then
and tear the young psychopath
    from his model heist.
    I was the paragraph.
    Constitute nothing
    worth stealing
    and then, when
    least expected, open
    the starting box
        and send out
        your voice.

About audiences,
the circle gathered round.
The thing is, those boys
that ran past, they also –
even with exceptional husbandry,
high rates of mastitis and also
mange. Strands,
audible. Prefers to draw on
skin rather than
paper. Floating back
to the surface of the day's
abstraction. Still,
the tilting of the football
field. Also, just
grass. The year never vanishes,
only seems to have gone
quicker than it took, also floating –
back to the surface
of the year's abstraction.
Capture the flag on the run
of paths through the trees,
voices as pondweed.
I sat alone
in the clearing.
Everything was also there.

light circles
   in the in the

    morning after
tree roots

lightning
   for sleep

    wire, ceramic
cork, fire

and singing
   a burn

Teachers' power to discipline pupils includes the power to discipline pupils even when they are not –

Even when they are older, ruined, alone, melding vague memories of something violentish with detritus from among the verge grass.

Nothing changes, except what hurts gets more, and people supposed whole wander around in ruins: schools, streets, parks, woodland.

Outside, in the corridor, Martin bellows, smashing all of the locker doors shut and open, shut and open like cymbals. A clattering grid.

Martin, who must scream in pain. Whose pain cannot be regulated. To whom every surface is as sounding brass, or a tinkling cymbal.

Martin, whose mask is unsalvageable. Whose mask crucifies his face. Whose face is spread out all across his skin.

Martin, whose visible order is stapled, deranged, to his hollers. Who goes in sorrow without relief, from freefall to the thumbscrew windpipes played by clowns in academic hats. Who runs home always inside himself alone.

Martin, who has within the forest in terrible spirals, opening, closing, dark and deep, and infinitely inward. Who has within its people, its terrorised dwellers, its agony of mindless questers moving ceaselessly with sharp edges under bruise tarpaulin and briar architraves.

Every day I come in here in my adult clothes and feel the shame of a child. The uncertainty of a child. The desire to communicate of a child. Delinquent flickerings.

SUMMER

DREAMLAND 3

There is
informed silence
along the causeway
where a figure
made of water
is dragging its feet
to St Mary's Church,
past the transfixion
of the priest
and the astonishment
of the square.
Breaths
die exploding
in the cold afternoon.
Some land
just has
treasure in it.
I see it now.

KILLING AGRAVAIN

There's a pale melody streaming
down a disused railway track
and a tracery of hedgerows
on the old green giant's back;

every village, every chapel
has a jewel in its throat
and cataracts of cloud mist up
the glass eye of the moat;

there are devils in the woodwork,
there's woodworm in the brain,
there's fencing in the phantom
of a whole half-day of rain;

a telescope will tell you
that the far end of the lane
is where you need to get to
when you're killing Agravain.

*

There's a brace of pheasants fleeing
through the thin hair of the king
and the faint trace of a circle
in the dead red kite's left wing;

in my hand there is a message
but the sender is deceased
and the woods are full of blood because
the dogs have been released;

there are peacocks in the palace,
there are placards that explain
that the horrors that have passed this way
will pass this way again;

a knight may well be pricking
and be pricking on the plain
but pricks are for beheading
when you're killing Agravain.

*

I thought in the beginning
that his face would start to shine
when the LiDAR scan of Cornwall
scorned the crops and lit the line

but the flesh can be deceiving,
all the more when underneath
is a skull that's gone to ruin
and two rotten rows of teeth;

there are bodies in the closet
and my lady doesn't know;
the ones who used to seek me
are the first ones now to go;

a word can be a bullet
that has nothing at its heart,
like the nothing that remains
when Agravain is blown apart.

In sleep, it's octane.
Wave-fire of red alarm.
Nothing to say here.

Things begin to converge on the pond
glades and familiars, refractory and
undissolved through days. Summer is
the same way Spirit helps us in our week
or kestrel lines and unimprovable
pleasure: to The Bevy to buy flowers.
Ross; beard; laughing; and upstairs
steam folds baffled from the window
picking stitches with Kat, forehead
to forehead, as May falls down beside.

everything buttercups
and white-stippled green
lows like running laughter
flying forward, backward but
from waving lines a hot balloon
rage-buttered Greg
of white leaf flow through
barbs and spits out
bullets of his wounded hull
rejection is a drift
that reaches uselessly and losing them in gas
its chimney-tips
today you will see me
hurt to be seen

W/C 5 JUNE

So, this is what time
    has come to

hopping ahead of me
    up Hollingbury hill

flightless on the side of
    the Iron Age.

In the orchard's skirts
    May lapses towards

a pear, pregnant, golden
    tolling in the bough

and blossom blubbing
    in the river's heads.

This time, I was exalted
moving forward through the day
like the prow of a ship
and, as I glided off
into the mists which made
no horizon, attention slipped
backwards like a rivulet
to the plateau
fatigue
rising perfectly compact
in the model terrain,
emerald green with delicate
small trees, that held
the classroom together.

DREAMLAND 4

I see it now.
     The ruin
   of an abbey,
    the rich green
of a riverwalk,
     the ceiling
    of a barn,
as beautiful as vaulting
   that beat the blue sky
     at its own game.
     An aeroplane
or dawn finding the sun alive.
    The bed
is too small for me,
   the room is too
   cold for me,
     the sky
     is too wide.

The spider opened
on my hand, the yellow

flowers that came true
in twilight, late

an hour since
we left them. Touch

is closer to the ground
than sight.

w/c 4 july

Heat builds
in a solid wave, remembering
more or less nothing
in a red dress: free
evening, the sea the fire
of grapefruit, an image
in my head
like a new glass wind.

Kat says, if I were buried I'd have my gravestone be the form of a door.

Saturday. Unseasonal mildness. Nothing but blue sky, leaves shaking their shadows down onto our cheeks. A woman called Julia appears beyond the fence. Was it you who crushed my blackberries with this door? Did you put this door here?

Her calm, but that calm, over there. The river of my verving free. Paddock on the desk, side-eye. Time and the hour. What is school but. Saying you. Sliced off forever! Paddock. Your familiar you – I. Your familiar is – yes. That part of you you cannot hold within yourself, yourself. As part of you. Yourself apart.

KENT

Starting on Monday
and then Tuesday
we see nothing. A father
and son look up as we enter
their Hailsham shop.
Click.
A smile.
The pasty light
of a fishing lantern.
We take that for the van.
A mile or a half-mile
further on, we stop
to have our picnic
in the lee of a pylon

and in view of the cattle.
Past Battle,
the road is the flat of a golden
sword laid on Wealden
mud,
going down gently and
still more down.
The light
dulls at a roundabout,
a roundabout
at the edge of town:
Lydd.
Still nothing. No sand.
Dungeness. Out

there, we meet the estate

manager, Owen. Straight
away: the wives sunbathing,
the husbands fishing,
the children off,
bored,
flinging shingle
through windows like light.
Cars, brink-
parked, sink
into that same shingle
and I'm blamed. He pauses to cough.
I'm ignored.
And the *mink*...

Next day,
among the dawns of gorse made honey
by the sun, the first
clue. A cursed
mink confronts
us, while,
from Dungeness B,
strokes light
against the sky,
a pylon strides by.
Perhaps this man's a dad. We
can only assume. Once
he's gone he is still there. While
my

efforts fail like young men
flung from rigging off Singapore, Owen
had finished,
fished
from the sea – or not –

and commemorated
in the cold
light
of regret, the desert flowers glow
unwitnessed. Well, blow
us down. An old,
grey gravestone shot
with rust at All Saints' Lydd.
Some Joe

extinguished just like that
and a primrose burning splat
in the stone's frame.
The name
Northfleet, too,
a Blackwall frigate
skewered by the *Murillo*,
Dungeness light
ablaze to no end,
too blind
to witness the still, slow,
frozen wave alive with clues
go down in a spate
of waves. Send

for help – there are
fathers and mothers spent here
uselessly. With the
corner
of our eye, we seize
the pylon dashing past –
giant pilgrim,
light
source. Canterbury.

The road the flats of gladii
laid in slim
succession down centuries.
We have breakfast
in sight of the heart of the see.

In the mote-lit air,
flags dissolve. Spare
time bleeds over caught
time, time caught
in graffiti's counterscript:
PBIG 1603, I Goings 1749,
WT 1768
and, in light
lines, Sean + Julie 2001.
Then,
as now, the long drape
of stone, the crypt
the shrine
of each self undertends,

the abstract
agedness of the texture of a flat
life. The cathedral's
stalls
purpled, redded,
rendered golden by
the freefall
of light
through incomprehensible
stories, the miracle
of Thomas Becket and the initial
LEGO brick, Eustace reunited
with his family
in a brazen bull

and, before that, watching lions
kidnap his sons,
straddling two shores,
a pylon. Scores
of French kids flood
the Corona
but the martyrdom was corner-
born, out of the light,
where a body could be
riddled in its secrecy,
not openly destroyed before
God
as waterfalls of stone
and tall, blotchy

mouths of glass.
We see a shadow pass
behind the windows,
fast at first. It slows
to shade.
The sun
shines on,
points of light
catch the achievements
of the Black Prince,
golden
gauntlets and so on, remade
for the long run.
Moments

go by.
Suddenly,
a giant's fistful
of shingle

bursts through the stained
panes, turning
a swathe of multicoloured
floorlight
white. In volcanic fury,
we upheave from our TV.
Dullard
children again,
spurning
their wretched family –

mum sunbathing,
dad fishing –
to excruciate
the good denizens of Dungeness estate.
But we only see, beyond
a sawtooth edge
of many-coloured glass,
a pylon in the light,
listing to port
like a Blackwall frigate,
spilling a glissando
of pebbles from its hand,
then hopping over the next hedge
to make good its get

away like a bad dad.
Sad.
What remains? Low, strange childrens
of lichen
shifting in the drift,
vacant tourists

drifting across shingle
in the *special* light,
the estate manager, Owen, fed
up – he states simply: sods –
and a single
grief, like a ship's whistle
in watercolour, mist-
bloodied.

DREAMLAND 5

There is
Little Red Riding Hood
under the bridge,
shaking,
shaking.
There is
an ogre
under the bridge
spewing
a river-beard
of fast froth,
shaking the bluebells,
shaking the whole world.
This is the space
of deterioration,
of dieback
in a lightshaft.
I see it now.

ACKNOWLEDGMENTS

Versions of these poems have appeared in *Anthropocene*, *bath magg*, *berlin lit*, *Blackbox Manifold*, *Chicago Review*, *The Junket*, *Ludd Gang*, *PN Review* and *Poetry Review*. Many thanks to the editors!

'Paddock calls', the 'Corridor Fragments', 'Eating a Bacon Bap at Carat's' and 'Door' first appeared as parts of *Paddock Calls: the Nightbook*, published by Owen Brakspear's slub press – so much gratitude to him for his commitment to making books and community.

'Dreamlands 1–5' were published as the third instalment of Earthbound Poetry Series Volume Five – thanks to Ian Heames for involving me in that beautiful project.

Love and thanks to Kat Addis, Andy Breckenridge, James Burton, Hugh Foley, Isabella Hammad, Will Harris and Joseph Persad for affirmations of, and wise suggestions about, the book-in-progress; to Kelly Ballett for the cover drawing; and to everyone at Carcanet, especially John McAuliffe, for their input and ideas.

An audiobook – not of the letter but of the spirit – of *Answerlands* is available at
https://josephminden.bandcamp.com/album/answerlands